Terms and Conditions

LEGAL NOTICE

The Publisher has strived to be as accurate and complete as possible in the creation of this report, notwithstanding the fact that he does not warrant or represent at any time that the contents within are accurate due to the rapidly changing nature of the Internet.

While all attempts have been made to verify information provided in this publication, the Publisher assumes no responsibility for errors, omissions, or contrary interpretation of the subject matter herein. Any perceived slights of specific persons, peoples, or organizations are unintentional.

In practical advice books, like anything else in life, there are no guarantees of income made. Readers are cautioned to reply on their own judgment about their individual circumstances to act accordingly.

This book is not intended for use as a source of legal, business, accounting or financial advice. All readers are advised to seek services of competent professionals in legal, business, accounting and finance fields.

You are encouraged to print this book for easy reading.

Table Of Contents

Chapter 1:
Introduction

Chapter 2:
How To Succeed In A Clickbank Business

Chapter 3:
Soft Skills Applicable In Clickbank Industry

Chapter 4:
10 Things Anyone Should Know About Clickbank

Chapter 5:
Comparison Of Clickbank And Other Marketing Strategies

Chapter 6:
10 Reasons Why Everybody Should Be OnClickbank

Chapter 7:
The Ultimate Goal One Should Have When OnClickbank

Chapter 8:
The Most Successful Case Studies

Chapter 9:
Special Places To Go On Clickbank For YourProduct Advertising

Wrapping Up
Things You Will Need To Know About HostingClickbank Sites

Foreword

Clickbank is one of the ways you can earn money from the Internet. You probably will have a hard time believing such a statement; perhaps you have tried it before and it did not work for you. But it is possible that you just haven't tried the best strategies available, and thus experienced the disappointment. Get all the info you need here.

Clickbank Cash Cow Secrets
Monetize The World's Biggest Marketplace Today!

Chapter 1:
Introduction

Synopsis

In this ebook Clickbank Cash Cow Secrets - Monetize the World's Biggest Marketplace Today! you will learn a systematic and foolproof way of turning Clickbank into a gold mine. It won't be difficult because it's true: Clickbank is really the biggest marketplace nowadays.

What You Get From the Book

The book is composed of 10 chapters and in each one of them, you will learn from people who have used Clickbank to make a big difference in their financial situations.

Chapter 2 of the book provides you with valuable tips on how you can succeed with Clickbank. The tips are commonsense but no less effective and do not demand from you a lot of complicated and costly things.

Chapter 3 teaches you how to communicate. This is the weakness of most Clickbank campaigners; they employ hard-sell techniques when they have been proven ineffective. In this chapter, you will be taught the intricacies of soft selling techniques and other techniques that bring in much needed sales.

Chapter 4 provides you with 10 essential pieces of information about Clickbank, its features and how they work, which you can use as resources for developing effective affiliate marketing campaigns or direct sales promotions.

Chapter 5 provides a comparison between Clickbank and other affiliate marketing outfits and the capabilities of each in terms of earnings, cost and ease of implementation. In this chapter you will see that it's Clickbank that offers the best chances and opportunities for earning a respectable amount of income from the Internet.

Chapter 6 offers you ten reasons why when you are thinking of obtaining supplemental income or thinking of selling something over the Internet, there is no other place to go but Clickbank. You do not actually need that second job to make ends meet.

Chapter 7 helps you develop your ultimate goal when you are using Clickbank. A goal keeps you focused and focus is one of the main elements in obtaining success. You will learn how to add value to your efforts.

Chapter 8 offers you successful Clickbank case studies from which you get lessons that will help you avoid pitfalls and take a direct path towards success. These case studies will teach that when you persist, things will turn out well in the end.

Chapter 9 helps present Clickbank campaigners increase their traffic. This chapter tells you where to go and what to do to address the problem. Marketing is all about traffic, so you will find the information provided in this chapter very important.

Chapter 10 provides tips to help you find the most effective sites to host your promotional blogs. There are many such sites and you will save a lot of research time and trouble later on by going directly to a site proven to offer the best hosting services.

Hitting Two Birds with One Stone

Going into affiliate marketing to earn supplemental income during your free time is as good as other ways of earning money from the Internet, maybe even the best because at Clickbank there are literally thousands of products you can sell and commissions can go as high as 50% of cost.

All you need to do is find your niche, a product you can promote with authority, and you have won half the battle. And you will learn about all of that in the book.

Clickbank is also the best place to market your own product because after all, you have the assistance of thousands of affiliates. While you are at it, you can do your own affiliate marketing on the side. You hit two birds with one stone.

Registering with Clickbank is simple: click the registration, fill-up the blanks and you are all set. If you want to make Clickbank make a difference to your finances though, don't forget to read the book.

Chapter 2:
How to Succeed in a Click Bank Business

Synopsis

Before, it was quite hard to imagine integrating marketing on the Internet, but intelligent and dedicated individuals made it happen. Today, people that were very much interested in making money on the web are now afforded opportunities to do so through Internet marketing, writing and editing, and other ways. These three are the most popular ways to make money online, but there are other ways for people to make money on the web though Internet marketing is the most effective way.

Although there are a lot of ways to make money online, Clickbank is the one that should be considered as the best. It is regarded as one of the simplest marketing websites today, especially if you have some background in Internet marketing. The thing that makes Clickbank one of the best is the fact that it is the perfect place to advertise due to the leniency it gives to affiliate marketers. What's more surprising here is that most sellers on the website provide high commissions for affiliate marketers – this is a great treat for people who know a thing or two about marketing.

However, success with Clickbank takes more than just knowledge in Internet marketing. Therefore, this article will give out some invaluable tips to help affiliate marketers find success with Clickbank.

Simple and Effective Tips for You to Succeed at Clickbank

Be Forum Visible

First off, you will need to look for forums where people who are involved with your niche spend time. For instance, if you are advertising or selling eBooks that directly help car enthusiasts from around the world, then you should look for forums that talk about cars and nothing else.

Additionally, most forums will allow signatures on the bottom of each of your posts, so you might as well utilize this leniency and advertise all you want.

As discussed earlier, you should be looking to post relevant topics and information on the forum. Don't make off topic posts just for the sake of advertising the things that are contained in the signature portion. Be as friendly as possible so that people may accept you with open arms, because if you do otherwise, you will risk getting banned from that forum and all similar forums.

Expose Your Brand

It is best to affix your unique signature in emails which includes a link to your business or sales website. Even if your email does not mention

anything about your business or product, your recipient will be curious enough to click on it to know more about what you have to offer.

In case you are into email marketing as well, be sure to fill the emails with some of your advertisements so that when people read their mail, they will see the products and services you provide.

That said, emails should also contain content that interests people so that they will read your emails and if you're lucky, they may even share it with their friends. Again quality content and relevant topics play a big role with your marketing strategies.

What you should remember here is that instant success cannot be attained through Clickbank, but if you have the right attitude and the right methods, you will make some money through the site in less than a month.

Chapter 3:
Soft Skills Applicable in Clickbank Industry

Synopsis

For those who are hearing of "soft skills" for the first time, you may know of it under a different name. Others also refer to it as the skills that make up a person's emotional quotient or EQ, as opposed to hard skills, which make up the basis for a person's IQ or intelligence quotient.

Soft skill training is essential even in the Clickbank industry. Some may argue that most soft skills – like communication for instance – would prove useless in a virtual world. That is patently untrue though. Communication still matters even if you are selling products online. You still need to communicate with your target market. The only difference this time is the platform you are using to communicate.

What Soft Skills Do You Need for Effective Clickbank Marketing?

In general, many types of soft skills can prove essential when you have something to promote in Clickbank, though some skills may be more important than others depending on your product and marketing strategy.

- **Personality traits** – Are you a *funny* person or are you entirely too serious? Such traits can greatly affect how you approach your customers online and even how your product write-ups would come out.

- **Social graces** – Simply put, being able to display *good* manners at all times is a skill in itself. It may not seem so, but your customers will appreciate how courteous and polite you are in all your dealings.

- **Communication** – Of the many soft skills there are, this is arguably the most popular, but unfortunately one of the most difficult to master as well. Some people are lucky enough to find communicating with others easy, a skill that they're born with. But others are not as fortunate and need to work twice as hard to be eloquent and convincing. Either way, it is a skill that you must not be complacent about.

- **Personal habits** – Whether or not personality traits are inherent and fixed or not is still debatable, but there's no such ambiguity when it comes to one's personal habits. These are

activities that you cultivate over time due to frequency. They are habits you can "un-learn" or eradicate from your routine with enough time, effort, and determination.

- **Friendliness** – Yes, friendliness is a soft skill in itself and one you can hone over time. However, you can be better at cultivating *and* maintaining friendships if you focus first on learning and appreciating the benefits of friendship – without any ulterior motives. People won't want to be friends with you if they see that you just want something from them.

- **Optimism** – This may also come as a shocker at the start, but if you think about it really hard you'll realize that being optimistic at all times can be hard work. You may not be born optimistic, but you can get around that by deliberately training yourself to become a *positive* thinker.

All the soft skills listed above will definitely help you achieve more of your Clickbank goals, but don't think that they are *all* the skills you need to succeed. Hard skills, technical skills, and other major types of skills matter, too, and will all definitely help in providing you with a well-rounded marketing strategy.

Chapter 4:

10 Things Anyone Should Know About Clickbank

Synopsis

In this modern era where everything is accessible online, Internet marketing has been one of the most profitable ways to earn money. This can be enjoyed by everyone from the comfort of their own home, which can allow them to better manage their time. If you are just starting to do Internet marketing, there is a certain website that will help you out: Clickbank. Get to know more about this network as you checkout the 10 things anyone should know about Clickbank.

Know This

1. Clickbank is a third party service that is able to link thousands of merchants in the World Wide Web. It is capable of providing you with the latest technology to deliver the campaigns and other promotional materials of the merchants. This service can also be described as an affiliate network wherein it performs a specific function of being an intermediary between merchants and other affiliates.

2. Clickbank now holds the largest database of affiliates with different marketing programs, making them the biggest affiliate marketplace on the web.

3. Aside from being an affiliate network, Clickbank also performs other services like collecting commission fees from a merchant and distributes it to affiliates involved in a specific program.

4. It has a high-end, innovative tracking system that is made for convenience and ease of managing your online business. This tracking system is one of the top in the list of marketing trends.

5. Clickbank can provide you with 100,000 affiliates to give you the needed growth for your business.

6. Like any other businesses, people want to deal with a company that is fair. Clickbank's success is not just due to its system but also to its fairness in the way that they process commissions.

7. It is free and the sign-up is as easy as 1-2-3. Once you get to sign-in, you can sell your products right away. With its

promotional page, the would-be buyers will be able to see your products and services in detail. This will surely boost your sales.

8. Clickbank works with you all the way through. It also promotes and even sells your products or services. At the same time, it does customer service to any queries given to your products. From their vast experiences and hundreds of affiliates, this service also offers you the latest marketing strategies that will surely help your business grow.

9. You will also need sales reports and any documents to see the progress of your business. Well, this service also sends the exact report and even sends you a paycheck 2 times a month, if you are an affiliate.

10. Starting is easy with Clickbank. Since it already holds 10,000 products that you can sell, you will be able to choose the products that will work to your advantage. Usually, these products are e-books.

These are the 10 things anyone should know about Clickbank. So if you want to start your own online business, you can count on Clickbank as your way to climb the ladder of success. With these offers, what can go wrong?

Chapter 5:
Comparison of Clickbank and Other Marketing Strategies

Synopsis

Although there is no doubt that Clickbank is the go-to site for affiliate marketers, it does not mean you should place all your digital eggs in one basket right away. Certainly, there is nothing wrong if you take the time to look for alternatives to Clickbank even if it is only to compare the site to its competitors and weigh their respective pros and cons. By knowing what other sites can and can't offer compared to Clickbank, you will be better able to appreciate the features of Clickbank.

What You Can Get from PayGear

Although PayGear is one of the newer kids in the block, it's making enough waves on the Internet to grab most people's attention. One of its major advantages is its more affordable price range compared to Clickbank. Other advantages worth checking out are listed below.

One Account for All

With PayGear, clients no longer have to create separate accounts for their vendor and affiliate needs. All your merchant and affiliate needs can be managed from a single account and control panel, which in many ways can be quite the time-saver for you. This particular feature also has a lot of potential, because in the future it may be expanded to allow your vendor and affiliate promotions to complement each other.

Payment Options

The keyword here is 'option'. With PayGear clients are given a variety of payment options to choose from, which presently includes credit card payments using your preferred processor, Google Checkout, or the ubiquitous PayPal. Having a lot of payment options available is always good for the business because it allows you to entertain more customers.

Customization

Some may say a checkout page is a checkout page, but that's like comparing a five-star hotel and a budget motel on the same scale or comparing apples to oranges because they are both fruits. With PayGear, you can *customize* your checkout page and – if you do it right – your customized design can do wonders for your sales.

Adding a personalized touch to your marketing strategy is always a good thing. It makes your customers feel more special and valued, which in return will encourage customer loyalty. Customized checkout pages also help build a more professional image and reputation for your business, which can attract more new customers.

Coupon Code Integration

Coupons remain today as one of the most popular promotional strategies in most industries. If you feel having coupon codes to offer will help you in your marketing strategy, then you will be glad to know that PayGear enables clients to integrate coupon creation with their incredible one-click system.

Automated Affiliate Payments

Computing commissions can be a headache – especially if you need to input figures manually. Even the smallest mistake can be a huge problem as it might make your affiliates think you are not being honest with them. Thankfully, that won't be a problem with PayGear,

which offers an option for automating affiliate commission cash-outs using the client's preferred payment program. You just have to configure percentage for commissions – you can choose up to 95% of sales - and the rest can be left to the site's automated system to take care of.

There are a lot of other benefits to enjoy with this particular Clickbank alternative, but as mentioned earlier on, it's better to see all of them with your own two eyes.

Chapter 6:
10 Reasons Why Everyone Should Be On Clickbank

Synopsis

In the world of Internet marketing, ClickBank does not need any kind of introduction due to its popularity.

In a nutshell, ClickBank is an online store that gives everyone the opportunity to sell their products on the website. Many see the website as an affiliate marketer's paradise because of the ad spaces it provides.

If you are interested in online marketing, you should give ClickBank a go as it provides affiliate marketers high commissions when making a successful sale. Here are other reasons that might convince you to sign-up with the popular website as soon as you can.

Why Be There

1. Through ClickBank, affiliate marketers are afforded the opportunity to earn commissions that can be as high as 75% of the total price of the product. Although all sellers there do not provide 75% commission, the lowest possible commission you can earn is 50% of the total price of the product.

2. The developers of the website give the chance for webmasters to integrate the search box of ClickBank to their web or blog sites. In the event that buyers find what they're looking for with the use of the said search box, you will have commission.

3. The advertisements found on ClickBank's website can easily be embedded on your web or blog site. Often times, they can be linked with the ads from Google AdSense but the ads from ClickBank provide higher profits.

4. One highlight that makes ClickBank quite unique is that affiliate marketers do not need any knowledge about the technicalities related to web hosting, designing and the like. Upon registration at ClickBank as an affiliate marketer, you shall be given a link. Thus, you will be able to make money even though you do not have a website.

5. As an affiliate marketer on ClickBank, you will be afforded the opportunity to edit the Meta tags, descriptions, titles and keywords of the products you are promoting.

6. With ClickBank, your personal information as an affiliate marketer will not be displayed on the product or even when the products are searched for by buyers. This allows you to maximize the opportunity by advertising as many products as you would like without displaying how much you will earn from the sale.

7. ClickBank offers affiliate marketers various ways of promoting the products, in addition to the website itself. First, the marketer may promote all the products displayed on ClickBank. Secondly, you may promote categories and the sub categories. Lastly, you may promote the keywords, meta tags and descriptions only.

8. ClickBank allows you to refer friends and other people you know with a referral bonus when they register under your name.

9. The website also allows you to hide the other affiliate links you are promoting so that they will not see that you are merely an affiliate marketer and not the direct seller.

10. Lastly, you may register to ClickBank without spending even a single penny and earn as much money as you can.

Money is not a matter in question upon registration at ClickBank as an affiliate marketer. The only things you need are dedication and time for you to experience the limitless moneymaking opportunities afforded at ClickBank.

Chapter 7:
The Ultimate Goal One Should Have When on Clickbank

Synopsis

If there is one thing you should aim for when it comes to earning from Clickbank then it is to take advantage of its larger-than-life numbers. The figures that Clickbank produces in terms of affiliate marketing or Internet marketing in general are *huge*---in a good way.

It does not matter either if you want to penetrate the Internet's #1 marketplace as an **AFFILIATE** or as a **MERCHANT**. The numbers will remain in your favor, and the only thing you need to do is to figure out a way to make them work for you!

Clickbank Affiliates: 12,000 Products to Market

Notice that the word 'choose' wasn't used, and that's because you do not really have to choose one product to market per se. You can choose a variety of them to start with if you feel that's what's best. And if not, there's no reason why you can't start from scratch again with another set of products to promote.

However, Clickbank strives hard to make it easier for affiliate marketers to choose the best products for them to promote.

- Products are sorted out according to different categories to help affiliates find their ideal "niche."

- Statistics are provided for *each* product. Such figures include the product's commission percentage for affiliates, initial earnings for every sale, and *gravity*. More about the last factor later.

- Unique and *encrypted* links for affiliates can be created in an instant

- Affiliates are given a system to use for tracking clicks and sales they generate

Gravity, by the way, is based on a formula that Clickbank uses for computing the number of unique affiliates that have sold the said product in the past eight weeks. A high gravity score means you are competing with a lot of affiliates for the same product – and vice versa.

Although a lot of people will advise you to go for products with low gravity scores, what's really most important is to find a product you truly believe in *and* with a gravity score that you are confident of your ability to handle.

Clickbank Merchants: 100,000 Affiliates to Sell Your Products

On the other side of the fence, product owners or merchants get to enjoy over 100,000 of the Internet's most promising and successful affiliates in search of new products to sell. Now, the trick to getting the best affiliates to sign up with your program is simple: you need to offer them a product that's guaranteed to generate sales.

In Clickbank, bestselling products are typically characterized by the following:

- Information that is unique or known only to a few
- "How-to" advice that will aid customers in earning more money and preferably more quickly than usual, too
- Personal experiences to share that will be of value to customers or readers?

Many people think it is easier being a product owner than an affiliate marketer. While that may be true, it does not mean a merchant's life is without its own challenges. For one thing, you need to make sure that you have chosen the ideal commission percentage for your affiliates. Something too high can drastically hurt your sales while something too low can discourage affiliates from signing up with your program.

Chapter 8:

The Most Successful Case Studies

Synopsis

The great thing about case studies is that you get to prove which works or not with completely validated results. After all, you were the one who handpicked the elements used for the case study and you were the one who performed all of the steps. You were there to see how things progressed from scratch. And with Clickbank, you can certainly try out a case study of your own as well. Just be sure to keep the following pointers in mind.

One Model at a Time

Admittedly, there are more than a few existing models which have proven successful for those who want to make it big in Clickbank. Of course, they vary from each other in any number of ways. Some of them may be more complicated while others may require more cash injection than you're able to provide.

Obviously, you should choose what you feel most comfortable and confident about. But the one thing you should really keep in mind is to **work with one model at a time.**

A Case Study on Niche Marketing in Clickbank

For your own case study, here is something that will help you discover your moneymaking niche in Clickbank.

How to Find a Money-Making Niche

A *niche* can be defined as a group of people – which will serve as your target market – that share the same hobbies or interests as well as problems. In order to choose the best niche, just perform the following steps.

1. Check out the list of product categories in Clickbank. Choose at least 10 categories that appeal to you the most.

2. Research these categories one by one. Find out which ones are the most *profitable*.

3. Consider the *gravity* when choosing a product under a category you have selected.

With these three steps, you'll have an easier time coming up with 10 products that you are most confident and comfortable selling.

How to Measure Niche Popularity

Google is your best friend here or – more particularly – its external keyword tool. Determining the most popular keywords in your niche will help you discover the following:

- The size of your market
- The type and size of competition you are up against
- Related keywords that your competition hasn't used yet

How to Measure Niche Probability

A niche can be popular without being profitable. In order to ensure your niche has the capability of generating sales, you need to focus on these three factors.

- Sales Potential – If advertisers are spending tons of money on advertising in your niche, then it only means they see money-making opportunities in it.

- Affiliates – What merchants earn are different from what affiliates get from commission. Affiliate earnings will be much smaller if there are too many of them already for a small niche.

- Entry Barriers – What other things could prevent you from penetrating your niche market successfully?

The Best Type of Niche Website to Create

Go back to Google and base your query on the following:
- (Your keyword) comparison
- (Your keyword) results

Your goal in this step is simple: you need to determine what kind of site works best in your niche. Examples of sites commonly used by affiliates today have been listed below.

- Review and/or scam sites
- Bypass type – Customers "bypass" merchant site and download directly from the affiliate's site
- Standard affiliate site

Once you've completed all these steps, you will only be left with two other things to do: registering a domain for your sites and building content for them. With this case study, your goal is to make $200 from each niche site.

You should have an easy time replicating the system for every niche site you put up. See for yourself how simple and easy this system can be. If everything works fine, then you will be earning more or less $2,000 every month.

Chapter 9:

Special Places to Go on Clickbank for Your Product Advertising

Synopsis

While you may already have more than a few good ideas about where best to promote your products outside Clickbank, what about marketing that you can do within the site? Believe it or not, a lot of sales may be generated from Clickbank alone. Ultimately, it all depends on knowing what those "special places" are and how to maximize them.

Resource Listings from Other Products

The strategy you're about to learn may seem like fraternizing with your enemy, but you can also look at it the other way as helping each other for the "greater good". Or it could even be as simple as the all too true cliché of "if you can't beat them, join them".

To start with, look for the three hottest products at present in your category. Does your own product have a lot in common with it? Can your product be considered a complement of sorts to any or all of them? Most importantly of all, do you think your product deserves a "slot" under the list of *Other Resources* found inside the product?

If you answer 'yes' to even just one of the above questions, then you've found one of the best places on Clickbank to promote your product. The only thing left for you to do is to figure out a way to convince the other merchant to help you out. In most cases, offering one or a combination of the following can be considered a worthwhile exchange for a resource listing.

- Exchange of resource listing
- Exchange of subscription lists (provided that you have the authority or permission to do so)
- Perform SEO marketing for the other product owner

Paid Promotions

There's another and easier way to promote your products in Clickbank. It's the best shortcut because you are getting Clickbank itself to help you out. In other words, you just have to pay the site to promote your products to its affiliates. This is obviously not the most affordable strategy to use, but it's likely to have a better success rate compared to other Clickbank marketing strategies.

With paid promotions, you need to be more careful about the way you choose to market your products. Clickbank will do its best to make your products visible to the best affiliates. The site will also provide you with the necessary tools to help polish your ads. However, the one thing that the site cannot do is the most important thing you must do as well: come up with a targeted and successful ad for affiliates.

Other Special Places for Advertising Clickbank Products

Although promoting within Clickbank is a great strategy for product advertising, you must also give the same effort and attention to advertising your product elsewhere on the Internet.

- Website and blog – Always have a place to call "home" online where you can freely write about your products.

- Social networking sites – This is typically the starting point for building contacts and keeping them updated.

List building – In order to get people to subscribe to your list, you must come up with a great digital product that you can offer them for *free*.

Wrapping Up
Things You Will Need to Know about Hosting Clickbank Sites

You've finally come to the end of the line, and you're just *one step away* from starting your journey to Clickbank success. That one last thing you have to do to generate sales either as a product owner or as an affiliate marketer is to create a website – and preferably a blog as well – for yourself.

Every online marketer needs a place in the Internet to call "home", preferably with its own address rather than merely using someone else's. You get to enjoy a more professional image as well if you have your very own website and blog to promote your products or share your affiliate links.

To do that, you need a web hosting package. There are countless to choose from nowadays, but as a Clickbank user, you will need to prioritize the factors listed below.

Affordability

For most first-time Clickbank users, affordability is the most important factor to consider with regard to web hosting packages. However, do not think of this as advice to choose the cheapest package. Rather, it's best to focus on hosting packages that are most reasonably-priced.

Domain Purchase

This may not have anything to do with website hosting per se, but it should nevertheless be part of your package. This way, you can make a single payment every month or every year for continued use of your domain name and web space.

Website Setup

Most web hosts nowadays also offer free website setups, which basically means you do not need to know or understand any kind of web or programming language to build your site from scratch. This is a must, as it will save you a lot of time and headache. Remember: you are better off spending your time improving your Clickbank marketing strategy than trying to get through Website Building 101.

Blog Integration

This is also a must-have, as it will ensure that your customers only have to click a single link to visit both your site and blog. In this case, your blog will appear as one of the pages in your website even though it may have its own theme, layout, and settings.

Pre-Made Templates for Affiliate Marketing

This is particularly important to Clickbank affiliates and would be a great help if you are promoting more than one product, but all of them have enough similarities to be marketed in a single place. Templates, however, must also be easily customizable.

Scripts and Plug-ins

All the usual plug-ins and scripts must be available. And if there is something that you need to download elsewhere, your web host must make it easy for you to install it.

Auto-Responder

It would also be great if you were able to enjoy the use of your own auto-responder from your web hosting package. With auto-responders, you can ensure that people who take the time to contact you will receive an immediate response---even if it is automated initially.

User-Friendly Control Panel

Last but not the least, it would be best to ensure that your preferred hosting package will come with an easy-to-use control panel. Without it, your beautiful website will still remain unproductive as you are unable to set it up and manage it the way you want and need to.

www.ingramcontent.com/pod-product-compliance
Lightning Source LLC
Chambersburg PA
CBHW030534220526
45463CB00007B/2827